# MEET GEORGE & GERTRUDE GOOSE

### Brett Moyer

**Goose Gather Farm**

To Shai,
Always be brave like Gertrude!

Copyright © 2022 Goose Gather Farm

All rights reserved

The characters and events portrayed in this book are fictitious. Any similarity to real persons, living or dead, is coincidental and not intended by the author.

No part of this book may be reproduced, or stored in a retrieval system, or transmitted in any form or by any means, electronic, mechanical, photocopying, recording, or otherwise, without express written permission of the publisher.

ISBN-13: 9798841641049

Cover design by: Brett Moyer
Printed in the United States of America

*To George & Gertrude*

It is with great joy to meet George & Gertrude Goose of Goose Gather Farm. These two have always been known to be early birds.

With a tall black neck, big round body of soft brown feathers, and two big webbed-feet, George and Gertrude enjoy floating on the river. When George and Gertrude come up onto the rocks to dry off, their feathers give them such good protection as they blend in and can barely be seen.

George and Gertrude live on a green grassy lawn. They enjoy munching on the lawn and snacking on the left-over's from the corn-field behind their home. Farmer James is kind enough to leave some corn for them each fall.

The two lovebirds that mate for life came from Canada to America and found the weather at Goose Gather Farm the nicest.

With a booming honking noise, Gertrude tells George it is time to prepare their nest. As they waddle back up to their home at Goose Gather Farm, Gertrude begins to weave twigs and sticks together to build a warm home.

As spring arrives, our Canada Goose friends ready their nest so Gertrude can lay her eggs which contain her goslings. With the eggs well protected in the large nest and Gertrude and George always on the look-out, the eggs are safe and warm.

Gertrude Goose will spend a whole month sitting on her nest keeping her babies warm in their eggs as they grow inside. In fact, when she does decide to go for a swim and have a quick grass salad for lunch, she will even cover the eggs with a blanket made of feathers she has pulled out of her own down coat. What love from Gertrude!

As the eggs hatch, the baby geese chirp and are quick to learn to swim and eat just like mom and dad. They don't like to see litter near their favorite lunch spot and follow a healthy diet.

They enjoy exploring their world and enjoying the puddles after the spring rains.

Even as they grow larger,
they will still find protection
from any predators and
the spring-time rain under
the wings of Gertrude.

But the goslings are always hungry and are on the search for grass and left-over corn to grow big and strong. When not on the hunt for food, they are enjoying the sunshine while they nap.

They should avoid any human foods such as bread and not have any plastic bottles littering their home.

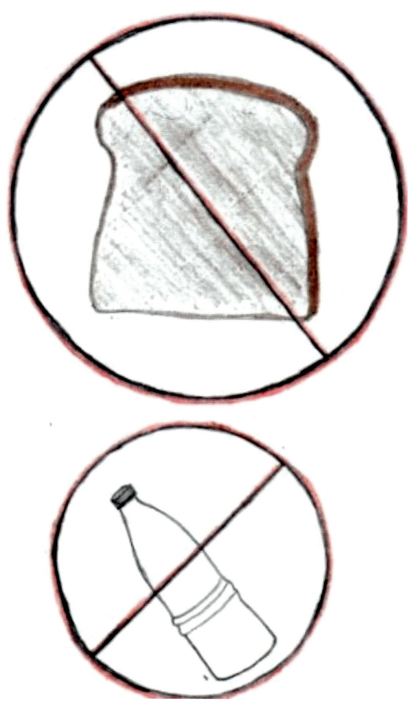

George and Gertrude are always close to them to teach them. Their goslings will be growing new feathers just as George and Gertrude grow new feathers of their own. This is called molting and you will often find old feathers scattered across the green lawn. The parents and goslings both will not be able to fly for nearly a month until they can have a fresh new set of wing feathers to show off!

But by the time the babies are grown and have feathers of their own, they are ready to take off to the sky. The goslings are excited to practice just like George and Gertrude as they get higher and higher off the ground.

Soaring hundreds of feet into the air, they fly as one big family in the shape of the letter V.  The V is not only Gertrude's favorite letter for VICTORY, but it helps them fly faster and further when they fly in that shape.

As they travel the lands, far and wide, they are always glad to return back to their favorite home of Goose Gather Farm. But until they return, let's keep their home safe and clean for them until we hear their honking in the skies!

Made in the USA
Middletown, DE
24 October 2023

41232243R00022